ST PETERSBURG

and Its Environs

Abris Publishers

St Petersburg

2002

Text by Alexander Margolis
Design and layout by Alexander Pompeyev
Edited by Alisa Veliurova
Translated from the Russian by Valery Fateyev

Abris Publishers thanks
the Peterhof State Museum-Preserve,
the State Hermitage, the State Russian Museum,
the Peter and Paul Fortress Museum of History and Culture
and the Russian National Library, St Petersburg,
for the kind permission to use their materials
in this book

Almanac: Treasures of Russia
Issue 49

Printed in Finland
Тираж 10000. Цена договорная
№ П 2462 в СЗРУ Госкомпечати РФ от 30.04.97
ISBN 5-88810-051-X

Peter the Great

The founder of St Petersburg

The Peter and Paul Fortress

The history of St Petersburg began on an islet near the right bank of the Neva, which became known as Hare Island. On 16 May (27 May Old Style) 1703, by order of Peter the Great, the foundations of a fortress called "Sankt Pieter-Burgh" in a Dutch manner, were laid there. The citadel was erected to protect the areas around the Neva taken by Russia back from Sweden in the course of the Northern War.

The fortress was the kernel from which the capital of the Russian Empire was growing and which gave to the burgeoning city its name – St Petersburg. The cathedral located on the territory of the citadel was named

The SS Peter and Paul Cathedral
Designed by Domenico Trezzini. 1712–33

after the Apostles Peter and Paul. Later the fortress itself also began to be called the Peter and Paul Fortress.

The first defensive structures of the fortress were made in wood and earth. The fortifications were designed as an extended hexagon with bastions at its corners and such layout made the fortress similar to "ideal" towns of the Renaissance. In 1706–40 the fortress was rebuilt in stone with the use of the newest achievements in the European art of fortification. During the early period the construction was supervised by the Swiss Domenico Trezzini, who became the first architect of St Petersburg. His work was continued by the German military engineer Count Burchard Christoph von Minich. In the 1730s two outer stone fortifications, the John and Alexei Ravelins, named after patron saints of the father and grandfather of Empress Anna Ioannovna, were put up at the flanks of Hare Island. During the age of Catherine the Great the walls and bastions of the fortress overlooking the Neva were faced with granite and as a result it has acquired a majestically austere and impregnable appearance.

The powerful vertical of the bell-tower of the SS Peter and Paul Cathedral crowned with a thin gilded spire vividly contrasts with the horizontally extended fortifications. The clear-cut silhouette of the fortress is especially imposing from the Neva, which soon became the city's main artery.

The Peter and Paul Fortress was made ready for combat several times, but it has never taken part in action throughout its history. Its destiny was different – to become the "Russian Bastille", the main political prison of Imperial Russia. One of its first prisoners was Tsarevich Alexis, the son of Peter the Great, who opposed his father's radical reforms.

In the 1920s, the Peter and Paul Fortress was converted into a museum. Today, various exhibitions of the Museum of the History of St Petersburg can be seen within its walls, and its stocks and research departments are located there.

The main entrance to the fortress is from Trinity Square, the oldest square in the city, by the John Bridge spanning the Kronwerk Strait.

The Peter Gate is a fine example of the early St Petersburg Baroque remarkable for its synthesis of arts (1714–18, architect Domenico Trezzini). Its entire decorative complex asserts, in an allegorical idiom, the stability of St Petersburg as a city protected by heavenly powers. The carved wooden bas-relief "The Magician Simon Cast Down by the Apostle", a work by the sculptor Conrad Ossner, is an allegory of the victorious struggle of Peter the Great against Karl XII of Sweden. At the top of the triumphal arch can be seen the

The Russian Imperial emblem over the arch of the Peter Gate

The Peter Gate. Designed by Domenico Trezzini. 1714–18

double-headed eagle holding the orb and sceptre, the emblem of Imperial Russia.

The arch of the Peter Gate is oriented directly to the east façade of the SS Peter and Paul Cathedral. The earliest place of worship in the northern capital, the cathedral is at the same time the burial place of the Russian Emperors, a memorial of a battle glory and a major court church (1712–33, architect Domenico Trezzini). Its bell-tower has become a sort of symbol of Russia's strengthening its position on the Neva and Baltic lands, the principal landmark of the entire city dominating proudly the flat terrain. It has remained the tallest architectural structure in St Petersburg (122.5 metres) to the present day.

The interior of the cathedral is designed as a vast state hall. Its prominent feature is the carved and gilded iconostasis notable for its light and dynamic forms as well as majestic yet elegant decoration (1722–29, Domenico Trezzini, Ivan Zarudny). The central part of this culminating accomplishment of the Petrine Baroque is reminiscent of a triumphal arch thrusting upwards.

The first Russian monarchs were buried in the Cathedral of the Archangel Michael in Moscow. After the construction of the Peter and Paul Fortress the burial place of the members of the Romanov Dynasty was moved to the SS Peter and Paul Cathedral in St Petersburg – nearly all the Emperors (except for the Tsars Peter II and Ioann VI) were buried there. The remains of Nicholas II, members of his family, their doctor and servants, who were shot in 1918 in Yekaterinburg, were interred in the Catherine Chapel of the cathedral on 17 July 1998.

To the east of the SS Peter and Paul Cathedral stands the massive building of the Grand Ducal Burial Vault (1896–1908, architects David Grimm, Anton Tomishko, Leonty Benois). Before the 1917 Revolution

The SS Peter and Paul Cathedral
The Tsar's Place

◀ *The SS Peter and Paul Cathedral. The nave*

Icon: The Almighty Entroned
1720s

The iconostasis of the SS Peter and Paul Cathedral
Designed by Domenico Trezzini
and Ivan Zarudny. 1722–29

Icon:
The Apostle
St Paul. 1720s

thirteen members of the Imperial family were buried there. In 1992 the great-grandson of Alexander II, Grand Duke Vladimir Kirillovich, was interred in the Burial Vault, and three years later the remains of his parents, Kirill Vladimirovich and Victoria Fyodorovna, who died in emigration, were also brought to the Peter and Paul Fortress from Germany.

In 1991 a monument to Peter the Great was installed in the fortress. It was presented to the city by the artist Mikhail Shemiakin who now lives in the USA. Drawing on the authentic representations of the emperor (he modelled the Tsar's head, for instance, on the mask taken by the sculptor Bartolomeo Carlo Rastrelli during the life of Peter the Great), Shemiakin created a grotesque image of the Emperor pervaded with power and energy.

Not far from the fortress, on the Peter Embankment running along the right bank of the Neva, visitors to the city can see its earliest surviving structure – the modest Cabin of Peter the Great. This cottage, fashioned out by soldiers of rough-hewn pine logs between 26 and 26 May 1703, is reminiscent of both Russian izba and Dutch dwelling house. Its two rooms, the Study

Icon:
The Resurrection
of Christ. 1720s

The tomb of Peter the Great

Icon: The Apostle St Peter. 1720s

*The SS Peter and Paul Cathedral
Tomb of the last Russian
Emperor Nicholas II
and his family*

*Tsesarevich
Alexis*

**Grand Duchesses:
Marie, Tatyana,
Anastasia and Olga**
(left to right)

Emperor Nicholas II

Empress Alexandra Feodorovna

and the Dining Room, are divided by the Corridor and
the Bedroom.

Already in the early eighteenth century the Cabin
was regarded as a historical relic. In 1723 it was protected by a stone gallery. Now it is encased within a brick
structure built in 1846. The museum display includes
personal belongings of Peter the Great and household
objects from his age.

*Monument to Peter the Great
By Mikhail Shemiakin
and Vyacheslav Bukhayev. 1991*

Vasilyevsky Island

asilyevsky Island occupying an area of 1,090 hectares is the largest island in the delta of the Neva. The eastern tip of the island, generally known as the "Spit", cleaves the deep waters of the Neva, like the pointed prow of a ship, into two branches, the Large and Small Neva.

In the middle of the 1710s Peter the Great decided to make Vasilyevsky Island the centre of his newly built capital and to provide it with a network of canals in the fashion of Amsterdam. The layout project was worked out by the architects Domenico Trezzini and Jean-Baptiste Le Blond. However, Peter's dream was not destined to come true – now only the geometrically straight ave-

nues and lines of Vasilyevsky Island recall this abortive attempt to create the Russian version of Amsterdam.

From the 1730s onwards the site was used as a sea port for a hundred years. Gradually Vasilyevsky Island developed into a scientific centre where almost all scholarly and educational establishments of the northern capital have been concentrated – the Academy of Sciences, the University, the Academy of Arts, the First and Naval Cadet Corps, the Kunstkammer, the Mining Institute and the Pushkin House (Institute of Russian Literature). Many eminent scholars and cultural figures lived in this "Latin Quarter" of St Petersburg.

In the early nineteenth century a magnificent architectural complex took shape on the Spit of Vasilyevsky Island. Its most prominent features were the majestic building of the Stock Exchange and the Rostral Columns – a world-famous architectural master-

◀ *View of the Spit of Vasilyevsky Island*
from the Palace Embankment

*The Stock Exchange
Mid–19th century. Coloured
lithograph by Jean Jacottet
and Aubrun from a drawing
by Joseph Charlemagne*

piece from the age of Classicism (1805–10, architect Jean-François Thomas de Thomon).

The tradition of installing rostral columns ("rostrum" means "prow" in Latin) as memorials symbolizing naval victories goes back to ancient Rome. The columns on the Spit of Vasilyevsky Island, thirty-two metres high, are decorated with rostra. Tradition has it that the four sculptures set up by the Rostral Columns symbolize the great Russian rivers: the Volga, Dnieper, Neva and Volkhov. The tripod bowls mounted at the top of the columns were used as lighthouses of the St Petersburg sea port – the bowls were filled with oil which was lit up in twilight.

In the early eighteenth century one of the most attractive features of Vasilyevsky Island was the estate of Prince Alexander Menshikov, Peter the Great's closest associate. The three-storey Menshikov Palace (1710–14,

The embankment at the Spit of
Vasilyevsky Island. Descend to the water

The Rostral Column at the Spit ▶
of Vasilyevsky Island

The University Embankment
The Menshikov Palace. Designed by
Giovanni Fontana and Johann Schädel
1710–14

◀ *The Spit of Vasilyevsky Island*
View from the Neva

architects Giovanni Mario Fontana, Johann Gottfried Schädel) by far surpassed all other buildings in St Petersburg of the Petrine age by its large dimensions and luxurious decor. It was in this stately edifice that lavish festivities and diplomatic receptions were held. In the course of its long history the Menshikov Palace was repeatedly extended and rebuilt. In 1731 it began to house a privileged military educational establishment, known later as the First Cadet School. In 1981 the palace has become a branch of the Hermitage Museum. The building itself and its restored interiors are the most important exhibits of this museum.

The building of the Kunstkammer, or Cabinet of Curious, is one of a few surviving monuments of the Russian Baroque (1718–34, architect Georg Mattarnovi, Nikolai Gerbel, Gaetano Chiaveri and Mikhail Zemtsov). In 1727, even before the construction of the imposing edifice was completed, it began to house a collection of "monsters and rarities" amassed by Peter the Great. Originally this first generally accessible museum in Russia contained under the same roof the library and observatory of the Academy of Sciences.

The main façade of the Academy of Arts (1764–88, architects Jean-Baptiste Vallin de la Mothe and Alexander Kokorinov) overlooks the Neva. Along with classes and studios the building contains a research museum of the Academy and a reference library. Integrally linked with the architectural complex of the Academy of Arts is the granite pier which embellishes the bank of the river (1832–34, architect Konstantin Thon). On either side of the stairway leading to the water are mounted, according to the architect's design, majestic effigies of sphinxes set on massive granite pedestals. The sphinxes are a thousand years older than the Neva River which emerged only 2,000 or 3,000 years ago. They were found during excavations in ancient Thebes, the capital of Egypt during the Middle and New Kingdoms. Carved of syenite in 1455–19 B.C., the sphinxes feature the head of Pharaoh Amenkhotep III and a lion's body. Brought from the banks of the Nile to St Petersburg in the spring of 1832, the mysterious mythological creatures became notable symbols of the northern capital of Russia.

The part of the bank remarkable for the pier adorned with the sphinxes was faced with granite in

The University Embankment
The Kunstkammer. Designed by
Georg Mattarnovi, Nikolai Gerbel,
Gaetano Chiaveri and Mikhail Zemtsov. 1718–34

*The University Embankment
Sphinx at the landing pier near
the Academy of Arts*

1843–44 when a construction of the first permanent bridge across the Neva began. This cast-iron multi-span bridge, designed by the engineer Stanislav Kerbiedz and called the Annunciation Bridge (now the Lt Schmidt Bridge), was opened for traffic in December 1850.

Downstream the Neva a proximity to the sea can be especially keenly felt. By the wall of the Lt Schmidt Embankment there are always plenty of ships. Cutters and tug-boats hurrying to and fro enliven the river landscape. A fresh wind from the Baltic Sea is blowing here most of the time. In front of the Naval Cadet Corps (1796–98, architect Fiodor Volkov) stands a monument to Ivan Krusenstern, who led the first Russian round-the-world expedition on the ships "The Neva" and "Nadezhda".

*The Lt Schmidt Embankment. Monument to Admiral
Ivan Krusenstern. Designed by Ivan Schröder
and Hyppolito Monighetti. 1870–73* ▶

View of the Admiralty. Ca. 1840
Tinted lithograph by Ferdinand Perrot

The Ensemble of Central Squares

Originally the central structure of St Petersburg on the left bank of the Neva was the Admiralty. The first industrial enterprise in the new city, the Admiralty shipyard was laid out according to a drawing by Peter the Great in November 1704. To protect the shipyard from the mainland, a fortress was erected around it in the autumn of 1705. Its earthen ramparts were provided with bastions and ditches spanned by drawbridges. Around the Admiralty fortress an extensive territory or esplanade was left bare and any construction was forbidden there for a long time. The space previously oc-

cupied by the esplanade can still be traced in the outlines of the squares which gradually took shape around the Admiralty (Palace Square, St Isaac's Square and Decembrists' Square) and are linked by Admiralty Prospekt. This historical part of the city where its political, business and cultural activities are concentrated is somewhat similar to the Forum of ancient Rome.

The focal point of this grand complex is the building of the Main Admiralty (1806–23, architect Andreyan Zakharov). The spire of the Admiralty glistening with gold and crowned with the image of a small ship became a symbol of St Petersburg as a sea gate of Russia. The Admiralty, unparalleled for the stateliness of its artistic image, compositional perfection and harmonious blend of architecture with monumental sculpture, ranks among the greatest works of Russian Classicism.

◄ *The Main Admiralty. Designed by*
Andreyan Zakharov. 1806–23

The formation of Palace Square to the east of the Admiralty was related to the construction of the new Winter Palace (1754–62, architect Francesco Bartolomeo Rastrelli). The palace is striking not so much by its huge dimensions as by its unusual luxury and elaborate decor which demonstrate the artistic principles of the Elizabethan Baroque of the mid-eighteenth century at its best. The square in front of the Imperial residence became the traditional place of military parades and festivities.

The architectural decor of the General Staff building (1819–29, architect Carlo Rossi), the construction of which was particularly important for the formation of the ensemble of Palace Square, is marked by the emphasis on its austere and concise features. The architect focused his attention on the centre of the composition – the majestic Triumphal Gate linking the main square of the city with Bolshaya Morskaya Street and Nevsky Prospekt. The arch is surmounted with the Chariot of Victory with six rearing horses (sculptor Stepan Pimenov and Vasily Demuth-Malinovsky).

In the centre of Palace Square stands a stately monument to Alexander I – the Alexander Column (1830–34, architect Auguste de Montferrand). This is one of the most grand architectural structures of this kind in the world. The height of the monolith of red granite is 25.6 metres, it weighs about 600 tons and the general height of the column including the figure of the Angel holding a cross is 47.5 metres.

Decembrists' Square which is widely opened towards the Neva, from the west is limited by a complex of buildings once occupied by the higher state establishments of pre-revolutionary Russia – the Senate and the Holy Synod (1829–34, architect Carlo Rossi). The focal point of the square is a monument to Peter the Great, the founder of St Petersburg, known as "The Bronze Horseman". The statue is cast of bronze after a model by the

Emperor Alexander I

◀ **The Saltykov Entrance
of the Winter Palace**

**The Arch of the General Staff building
Designed by Carlo Rossi. 1819–29
View of the Alexander Column**

Palace Square. The Alexander Column Designed by Auguste de Montferrand; the Angel by Boris Orlovsky. 1830–34

French sculptor Etienne Maurice Falconet. Peter's head was modelled by Marie Anne Collot, the sculptor's assistant. The memorial rests on a serpent trampled by the horse. The base of the monument is a huge granite boulder found on the shore of the Gulf of Finland not far from St Petersburg. The monolith was carved to be given the shape of a rock after a drawing by the architect Yury Velten. The base is inscribed in Russian and Latin: "To Peter the First from Catherine the Second". The monument was unveiled in August 1782. "The Bronze Horseman" ranks among the world's outstanding works of monumental art.

St Isaac's Square owes its name to St Isaac's Cathedral dominating it (1818–58, architect Auguste de Montferrand). The huge cathedral, 101.5 metres high, 111 metres long and 98 metres wide, is the largest church building in Russia. The fronts of the cathedral are faced with marble and granite and decorated with numerous

Decembrists' Square. Monument to Peter the Great ("The Bronze Horseman") By Etienne-Maurice Falconet. 1766–82 ▶

Unknown artist. Road on the Ice-Bound Neva
near Senate Square. 1867. Oil on metal

statues and bas-reliefs. The monumental porticos decorating its four fronts are remarkable for their columns carved of granite monoliths. The interior of St Isaac's strikes one by its grandeur and wealth of decoration. For the facing of the walls, pylons and iconostases various kinds of marble, porphyry, malachite and lapis-lazuli were used, and all of them perfectly blended with gilded bronze. The painted decorations and mosaics adorning the cathedral were executed by leading artists of the Academic school of the mid-nineteenth century. St Isaac's, completing the complex of the central squares, became the most important and dominant landmark in the silhouette of the city on the Neva.

In the centre of St Isaac's Square can be seen the fine monument to Nicholas II erected in 1856–59. The architectural solution of the monument belongs to Auguste de Montferrand. The mounted statue having only two points of support was modelled by the sculptor Piotr Klodt. The pedestal of the monument is decorated with reliefs which illustrate in an allegori-

View of St Isaac's ▶

The dome vault of St Isaac's

St Isaac's Cathedral. Designed by Auguste de Montferrand. 1818–58 Monument to Emperor Nicholas I By Auguste de Montferrand, Piotr Klodt, Robert Zaleman and Nikolai Ramazanov. 1856–59

Interior of St Isaac's ▶

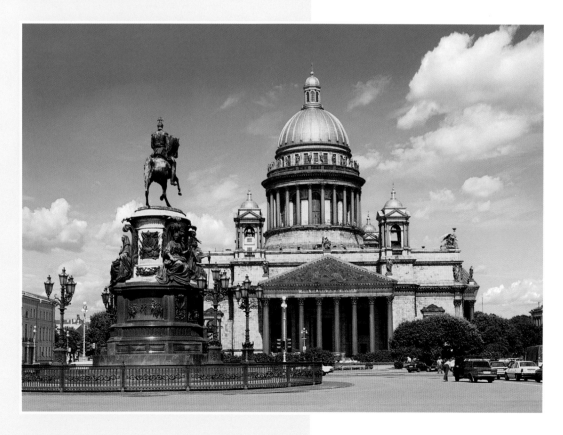

cal form various episodes from the history of the reign of Nicholas I (sculptors Robert Zaleman and Nikolai Ramazanov).

The space of St Isaac's Square is completed on the south side by the Mariinsky Palace (1839–44), architect Andrei Stakenschneider). The building was commissioned by Nicholas I for a young couple when his daughter Maria married the Duke of Leutenberg. In the late nineteenth century the palace was given to the State Council and now the Legislative Assembly of St Petersburg has its sessions there.

Emperor Nicholas I

**St Isaac's Square
The Mariinsky Palace. Designed by
Andrei Stakenschneider. 1839–44**

View of St Isaac's

The Palace Square
The Winter Palace. Designed by
Francesco Bartolomeo Rastrelli
1754–62

The Hermitage

T he Hermitage Museum, the largest repository of art in Russia and one of the most representative museums in the world, occupies several interconnected buildings on the Palace Embankment – the Winter Palace (1754–62, architect Francesco Bartolomeo Rastrelli), the Small Hermitage (1764–75, architects Jean-Baptiste Vallin de la Mothe and Yury Velten), the Old Hermitage (1771–87, architect Yury Velten), the Hermitage Theatre (1783–1787, architect Giacomo Quarenghi) – and the New Hermitage on Millionnaya Street (1842–51, ar-

◄ *The New Hermitage*
Portrico with Atlantes. Designed by Leo von Klenze;
the Atlantes by Alexander Terebenev. 1844–49

chitect Leo von Klenze). Moreover, the Menshikov Palace on Vasilyevsky Island and part of the General Staff building on Palace Square have also become the property of the museum.

The year 1764, when Catherine the Great acquired 225 paintings by Western European masters from the Berlin merchant Gotzkowsky, is considered to be the date of the foundation of the museum. Nowadays the stocks of the museum amount to about 3,000,000 exhibits ranging from works of painting, graphic art and sculpture to all sorts of decorative and applied art, artifacts, medals and coins.

To get acquainted with the displays of all the four hundred rooms and halls of the Hermitage, one must cover a distance of fourteen miles. Even if you stop in front of every exhibit just for a minute and spend eight

View of the Winter Palace during the Celebration of the Epiphany Day on the Neva on 6 January. Mid–19th century Coloured lithograph by Jean Jacottet and Aubrun from a drawing by Joseph Charlemagne

44

hours every day in the museum, it will take you almost fifteen years to see the whole collections.

Making a tour of the Hermitage rooms, you may find yourselves in Ancient Egypt, Mesopotamia, ancient Greece and its colonies on the northern coast of the Black Sea, familiarize yourselves with the ancient culture of the Etruscans and the primitive tribes of Siberia, to see Egyptian mummies, ancient pottery, a collection of Roman sculptural portraits, Scythian and Sarmatian artifacts.

Empress Catherine II

◄ *The Winter Palace. The Peter the Great Throne Room Designed by Auguste de Montferrand, 1833; Vasily Stasov, 1838*

◄ *The Winter Palace. The Main (Ambassador or Jordan) Staircase. Designed by Francesco Bartolomeo Rastrelli,1762; Vasily Stasov, 1831*

*The Winter Palace
The Malachite Room
Designed by
Alexander Briullov
1839*

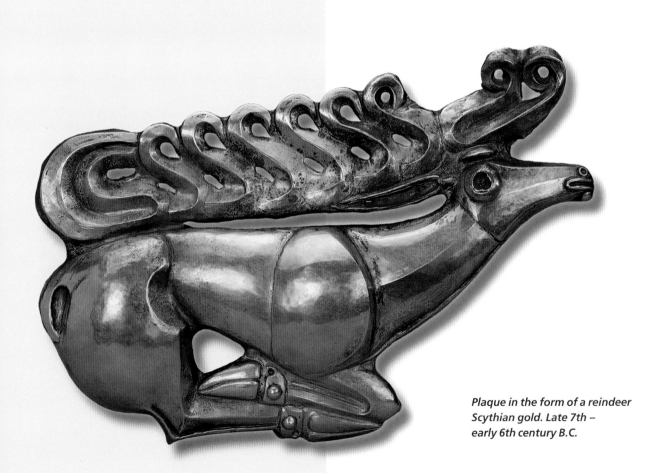

*Plaque in the form of a reindeer
Scythian gold. Late 7th –
early 6th century B.C.*

A gem of the Hermitage collection is the famous Gonzaga cameo. It was owned by Isabelle d'Este, the wife of Gonzaga, the Duke of Mantua, hence its name. The cameo is decorated with profile representations of the rulers of Hellenistic Egypt – Ptolemy II (Ptolemy Philadelphus) and his wife Arsinoë. The cameo, which is 15.7 cm high, is one of the largest gemstones in the world. The polishing of such hard stone as three-layered sardonyx demanded from the carver many years of work.

The Gonzaga cameo
Alexandria
3rd century B.C.

The Winter Palace
The St George (Great Throne) Room
Designed by Giacomo Quarenghi, 1795;
Vasily Stasov, 1843

The Small Hermitage
The Pavilion Hall
Designed by Andrei
Stakenschneider. 1850–58

The Pavilion Hall
Clock: Peacock
Designed by James Cox
18th century

The Large Carriage
France. 18th century

Leonardo da Vinci
The Virgin and Child
(The Litta Madonna)
Ca. 1491

The Old Hermitage
The Leonardo da Vinci Room
Designed by Andrei Stakenschneider
1858

Pieter de Hooch
Mistress and Maid
Ca. 1660

Peter Paul Rubens
Perseus and Andromeda
1620s

Rembrandt Harmensz van Rijn
Danaë. 1636

Willem Heda
Luncheon with Lobster
1648

53

The exhibitions of the Western European Department feature the art of Italy, Spain, Holland, France, Germany and Great Britain. Worthy of particular attention are canvases by great masters of painting from Leonardo da Vinci and Raphael to Henri Matisse and Pablo Picasso, sculptures, mediaeval arms and armour, tapestries, Italian majolicas, Limoges enamels and Sèvres porcelain…

Antonio Canova
Cupid's Kiss. 1796

Etienne Maurice Falconet, the French sculptor who was invited to Russia to create a monument to Peter the Great, had produced a large number of works earlier, during his life in France. The Hermitage collection includes his works covering the sculptor's most popular subjects. Falconet repeated his Cupid, one of the most popular subjects in eighteenth-century art, many times in a variety of materials.

The resplendent interiors of the Winter Palace and other buildings of the Hermitage, a masterpiece of Russian monumental and decorative art, are of especial value. These include such magnificent interiors as the Jordan Staircase, the Field-Marshal Hall, the Malachite Drawing Room and the Hermitage Theatre. Their decoration was carried out to the designs of such eminent architects as Francesco Bartolomeo Rastrelli, Vasily Stasov, Auguste de Montferrand, Alexander Briullov and Andrei Stakenschneider.

Etienne Maurice Falconet
Cupid. 1758

Jean Honoré Fragonard
The Stolen Kiss. Late 1780s

The New Hermitage. The Small Skylight Room
Designed by Leo von Klenze. 1840s ▶

The exhibition "The Winter Palace of Peter the Great" devoted to the founder of the city has been opened in 1992. It is located on the site of the former palace of the first Russian Emperor, the foundation and walls of which were discovered in the course of restoration of the Hermitage Theatre.

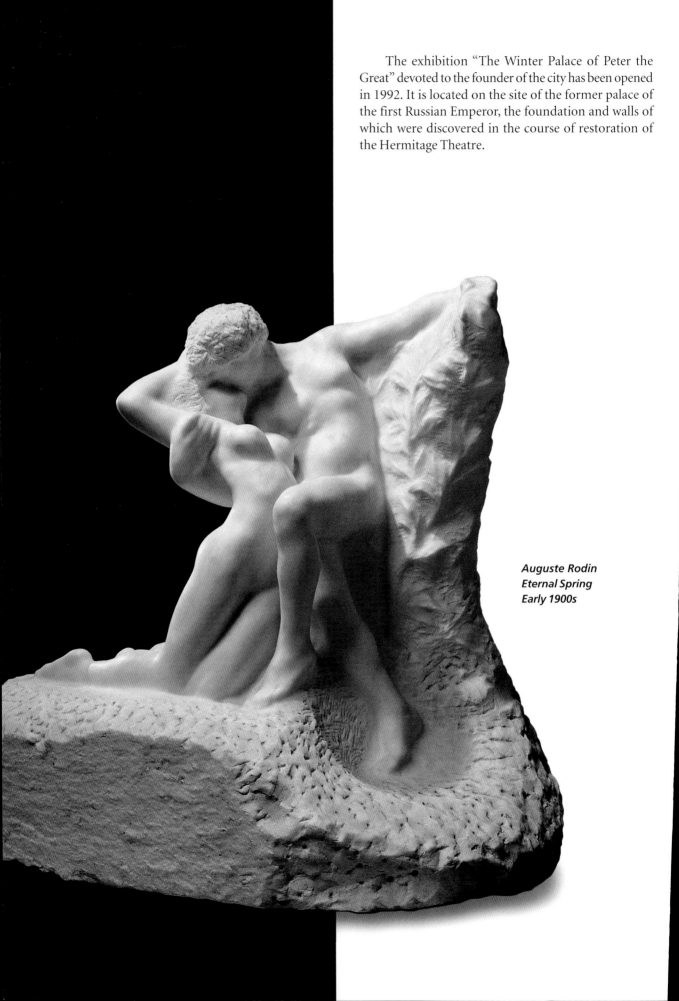

Auguste Rodin
Eternal Spring
Early 1900s

Vincent van Gogh. Cottages. 1890

Henri Matisse. The Dance. 1910

The Summer Palace of Peter the Great
Designed by
Domenico Trezzini and
Andreas Schlüter. 1710–14

The Summer Gardens

In the central part of St Petersburg, on an island formed by the Neva, Fontanka and the Swan Canal, is situated the oldest garden of the city with an area of 11.7 hectares. The gardens were laid out in 1704 by order of Peter the Great and to his original plan near his summer residence. The Summer Gardens, designed in a regular style (with a strictly geometrical layout of the avenues), was embellished with numerous statues, busts and fountains. The flood of 1777 destroyed the fountains of the Petrine age which were never restored. Out of 250 marble sculptures by Italian masters of the seventeenth and early eighteenth centuries only 89 have survived.

The austere and modest fronts of the Summer Palace of Peter the Great (1710–14, architects Domenico

Trezzini and Andreas Schlüter) are adorned with bas-reliefs featuring mythological subjects glorifying Russia's naval might. On the ground floor of the palace-museum visitors can see reception rooms, a study, a bedroom and a turnery of Peter the Great, as well as a dining room and a kitchen. The apartments of Catherine I on the upper floor include the Green Drawing Room where paintings, tapestries, furniture and objects of glass and porcelain dated from the age of Peter the Great are displayed. Although the palace was redesigned several times, the decoration of the vestibules and the oak staircase where clothes and other personal belongings of Peter the Great and Catherine can be seen.

The beautiful cast-iron railing of the Summer Gardens on the Neva side was created in 1773–86 (architect Yury Velten and Piotr Yegorov), and the railing

The Summer Gardens. The central avenue

Railing of the Summer Gardens from the Neva side ▶

on the Moika side was installed in the 1820s (architect Louis Charlemagne). On the territory of the garden are the pavilions, the Coffee House (1826, architect Carlo Rossi), the Tea House (1827, architect Louis Charlemagne) and a monument to the fable-writer Ivan Krylov (1854–55, sculptor Piotr Klodt).

The Summer Palace was the venue for Peter's famous assemblies, court festivities and receptions of foreign ambassadors. Until the end of the eighteenth century the gardens were accessible only to a narrow selected circle of royal dignitaries. Later it became a favourite place of recreation for the inhabitants of St Petersburg.

It is impossible to enumerate all prominent poets, artists and composers who mentioned the poetic Summer Gardens in their creative work. The gardens with their elevated blend of historical associations and artistic splendour are enchanting in any season of the year.

◄ *Statue: Apollo. Italy. 19th-century copy from a Roman original of the 1st century*

Unknown sculptor. Statue: Ceres
Early 18th century

Unknown sculptor Sculptural group: Cupid and Psyche. Italy Late 17th century

The Police Bridge. 1840s. Coloured lithograph
by G. Arnoult after a drawing
by Joseph Charlemagne

Nevsky Prospekt

evsky Prospekt is the main thoroughfare of the city. It was the most illustrious embodiment of the grandeur of the capital of the Russian Empire, the development of a capitalist city, the tragedy of the siege and the turbulent political life of the recent years. It is the focus of cultural life, business activities and public amusements. The largest museums and libraries, theatres and concert halls, shops and banks, hotels and restaurants are located on this street.

The appearance of Nevsky Prospekt is marked by an austere integrity and at the same time by a wealth of

The Cathedral of the Resurrection
("Our Saviour-on-the-Spilt-Blood")
Designed by Alfred Parland. 1883–1907

diverse visual attractions. The perspective of the thoroughfare is clearly oriented towards the tower and the golden spire of the Admiralty and its variety is further enhanced by picturesque rivers and canals, as well as by the wide squares which are visually connected with Nevsky Prospekt.

Nevsky Prospekt has embodied one of the most important features of the northern capital – its international character. On Nevsky Prospekt and next to it are concentrated main churches of different confessions and ethnic groups which inhabited St Petersburg. It is for this peculiarity that Alexander Dumas called Nevsky Prospekt "a street of toleration".

At the corner of Nevsky Prospekt and the Moika Embankment stands the Stroganov Palace, a fine monument of the Elizabethan Baroque (1753, architect Francesco Bartolomeo Rastrelli). Put up for Baron Ser-

Alexander Pushkin

gei Stroganov, the palace was gradually turned by its owners into a repository of various art collections, including those devoted to Western European and Russian painting. Between 1788 and 1793 the interiors of the palace were redesigned in the Classical style by Fiodor Demertsov and Andrei Voronikhin.

The palace was the property of the Stroganov family until 1917. After the revolution it was open for visitors as a historical museum of daily life, but later its collections were disintegrated. In 1991 the building became a branch of the Russian Museum. Nowadays reconstruction work is under way there and after its completion the palace will house an exhibition of decorative and applied art.

Upstream the Moika is one of the most museums St Petersburg – the memorial flat of the poet Alexander Pushkin honoured all over Russia. The poet spent the last four months of his life in the house No 12 on the Moika Embankment. He died in this flat on 10 February 1837, mortally wounded at a duel with Georges d'Anthès.

View of Alexander Pushkin's last flat in No 12 on the Moika Embankment

Unknown artist. The Lutheran Church of St Peter
Mid–19th century. Engraving on steel
tinted in watercolour

Visitors to the memorial flat can see the furnishings recreated according to the drawings done by Vasily Zhukovsky right after Pushkin's death. Of particular interest is the poet's study: his library, his writing desk, his favourite armchair and his bureau near a sofa. Hanging on the walls are portraits of Pushkin's friends, his wife Natalia and their children.

Usually churches were put up on Nevsky Prospekt with a recession from the street, and the front line was formed by symmetrical buildings belonging to church parishes. The German Lutheran Church of St Peter was built on Nevsky Prospekt as early as 1730. A new church, with two towers, an arcade and an imposing recessed façade, was built in 1833–38 to the design of the architect Alexander Briullov, who borrowed some elements of Roman architecture.

The opposite side of Nevsky Prospekt is dominated by the majestic Kazan Cathedral, a gem of Russian Classicism (1801–11, architect Andrei Voronikhin). The cathedral faces Nevsky Prospekt by its longitudinal side front. The architect concealed the main volume of the building by the immense colonnade of ninety-eight

Natalia Pushkina, the poet's wife

69

Nevsky Prospekt
The Kazan Cathedral. Designed
by Andrei Voronikhin. 1801–11
Monument to Mikhail Kutuzov
By Boris Orlovsky. 1831

Corinthian columns. His design is based on the pre-requisite of Emperor Paul I that it should be modelled on St Peter's in Rome. But the arc-shaped colonnade received here an absolutely different treatment – it is wide open and functions not as a subordinate element but rather as an important feature of the design playing, in actual fact, the role of the main façade.

In 1813 Mikhail Kutuzov, Commander-in-Chief of the Russian Army in the 1812 War against Napoleon Bonaparte, was buried in the cathedral. The building became a pantheon of military glory. The memorial significance of the cathedral as a memorial increased after 1837 when monuments to the Field-Marshals Kutuzov and Mikhail Barclay de Tolly (sculptor Boris Orlovsky) were unveiled in front of it.

An extensive tract of land on Nevsky Prospekt was allotted in the 1730s to the Roman Catholic Church of St Catherine. Two symmetrical buildings flank the recessed church which was put up in 1763–83 by the architects Jean-Baptiste Vallin de la Mothe and Antonio

*The Kazan Cathedral. Icon: St Nicholas
the Miracle-Worker. 19th century*

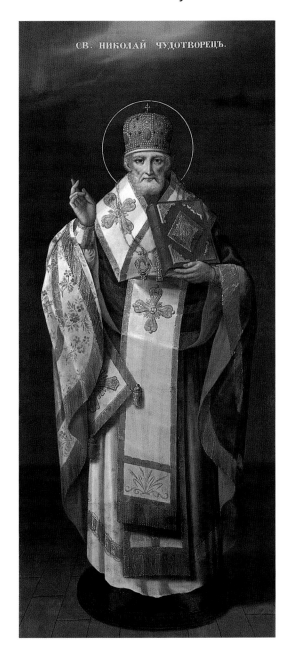

*The Kazan Cathedral. Icon: Our Lady
of Everduring Cup. 19th century*

*The colonnade ▶
of the Kazan Cathedral*

Rinaldi. The church notable for an immense arched portal, statues on the parapet and a tall dome is one of the best examples of the architecture marked by a transition from the Baroque to Classicism.

On the other side of Nevsky Prospekt soars the tower of the Municipal Duma (1799–1804, architect Giacomo Ferrari). This is the main, after the Admiralty, landmark of the thoroughfare. Once it served for optical communication between the Winter Palace and Warsaw, as well as a fire observation tower.

At the corner of Nevsky Prospekt and the Griboyedov Canal Embankment stands an imposing edifice with large windows attracting general attention by its elegant granite trimming combined with bronze decorations, and especially by a glass ball at the top of its tower which serves as an important accent in the silhouette of the street. The building was put up for the Singer Company, an American producer of sewing machines (1902–04, architect Pavel Suzor). After the 1917 Revolution the building has become known as the House of Books in which the largest book shop in the city and various publishing companies are located.

The Gostinny Dvor Shopping Arcade
Mid–19th century. Coloured lithograph by
Jean Jacottet after a drawing by Joseph Charlemagne

The Bank Bridge. Designed by Wilhelm von Tretter. 1825–26

To the south of Nevsky Prospekt, where the Griboyedov Canal makes its first twist, you can see the Bank Bridge intended for pedestrians. It was built in 1825–26 by the German engineer Wilhelm von Tretter. The chains of the suspension bridge are fixed on the structures hidden by the mythological griffins with gilded wings (sculptor Pavel Sokolov).

In the northern direction there unfolds a clear perspective of the upstream of the Griboyedov Canal, with a vivid round dance of the domes of the Cathedral of the Resurrection, commonly called "Our Saviour-on-the-Spilt-Blood". The cathedral stands out by its picturesque silhouette, bright varicoloured decoration and old Russian shapes sharply contrasting with architecture in the Classical style around it. The tower of the cathedral rises to the height of 81 metres.

The Cathedral of the Resurrection was built in 1883–1907 on the site where on 1 March 1881 the Emperor Alexander II was mortally wounded by a bomb thrown by the terrorist Ignaty Grinevitsky. It may be

Emperor Alexander II

said that "Our Saviour-on-the-Spilt-Blood" is a St Petersburg imitation of pre-Petrine ecclesiastical architecture with its centre in Moscow. The memorial cathedral in a "distinctly Russian" style was built to the design of Alfred Parland who borrowed many compositional devices and shapes from Moscow and Yaroslavl churches of the seventeenth century. The main volume crowned with five-domes is adjoined by the bell-tower with a gilded dome and two porches. The crowning features of the façades are kokoshniks (decorative arched gables) with fancy-shaped window surrounds and polychrome tiles.

In the centre of Ostrovsky Square is a monument to Catherine the Great erected in 1862–73. The monument was designed by Mikhail Mikeshin with the par-

The Cathedral of the Resurrection ("Our Saviour-on-the-Spilt-Blood") Designed by Alfred Parland. 1883–1907 ▶

Detail of the upper part of the Cathedral of Resurrection – a kokoshnik decoration with the mosaic composition "Christ the Pantocrator"

ticipation of the architects David Grimm and Victor Schröter. The towering statue of the empress (sculptor Matvei Chizhov) is encircled by sculptural representations of nine statesmen of her reign (sculptor Alexander Opekushin).

The culminating period of urban construction in St Petersburg were the first decades of the nineteenth century. It was in this period that the system of architectural complexes in the centre of the city took its final shape. The largest of them is creation of Carlo Rossi, the ensemble of the Alexandrine Theatre flanked by two squares connected by a street.

Further Nevsky Prospekt crosses the Fontanka River by the three-span Anichkov Bridge. In 1841–50, four

Mikhail Nesterov. Mosaic: Descent into the Limbo

◀ *Alfred Parland. Mosaic: The Crucifixion*

Nikolai Kharlamov
Mosaics of the ceiling cupola: "The Pantocrator"

sculptural groups with horses (sculptor Piotr Klodt) were installed on its granite pediments. Executed with a striking mastery and pervaded with dynamism, they make up an expressive sculptural ensemble. In the 1840s Klodt made replicas of the two groups from this complex for Berlin and Naples.

The bridge affords panoramic views of the Fontanka – the gentle curves of the banks clad in granite, of palaces and mansions, with the so-called Fontanka Mansion and the Beloselsky-Belozersky Palace particularly noticeable among them.

The elegant Sheremetev Palace or the Fontanka Mansion (1750–55, architect Savva Chevakinsky and Fiodor Argunov) is designed in the Baroque style. There is a regular garden behind the palace. In the 1840s

Monument to Catherine the Great
By Mikhail Chizhov, Alexander Opekushin,
Mikhail Mikeshin and David Grimm. 1862–73

The Alexandrine Theatre. Designed by
Carlo Rossi, Vasily Demuth-Malinovsky,
Stepan Pimenov and Antonio Triscorni. 1828–32

The Anichkov Bridge across the Fontanka
Sculptural group. By Piotr Klodt. 1841–50
The Beloselsky-Belozersky Palace
Designed by Andrei Stackenschneider
1847–48

◄ *The Fontanka Embankment*

a fine railing was erected in front of the main façade of the palace to the design of Hyeronimo Corsini. The Counts Sheremetev owned the Fontanka Mansion for more than 150 years and it was considered their patrimony. From 1990 the estate belongs to the Museum of Theatrical and Musical Art. The well-known poetess Anna Akhmatova lived in the garden wing of the palace for a quarter of a century. In 1989 her memorial museum has been opened in this building.

The palace which was owned by the Beloselsky-Belozersky family, affords views of both Nevsky Prospekt and the Fontanka. It has acquired its present-day appearance in the Neo-Baroque style as a result of alterations made in 1847–48 by the architect Andrei Stakenschneider. In the late nineteenth century the

palace was the property of Grand Duke Sergei Alexan-
drovich, the brother of Emperor Alexander III. Now
the building houses the cultural centre of the St Petersburg Administration.

The second part of the main thoroughfare of
St Petersburg, commonly called Old Nevsky Prospekt,
ends at the entrance to the Alexander Nevsky Lavra ("lavra" means a major monastery in Russian). The monastery was founded by Peter the Great in 1710 in memory
of the celebrated warrior of ancient Russia, the Prince
of Novgorod Alexander Nevsky, who was canonized.
Tradition has it that on this site he won his victory over
the Swedes in 1240 (in actual fact, however, the Battle of
Neva took place at the spot where the Izhora empties
into the Neva). The design of the monastery was worked
out by Domenico Trezzini in 1715, later the construction work was carried out by Teodor Schwertfeger, Pie-
tro Antonio Trezzini, Ignazio Rossi and Mikhail Ras-
torguyev. They created an imposing ensemble in the

The Fontanka Embankment
The Sheremetev Palace (The Fontanka
Mansion). Designed by Savva Chevakinsky
and Fiodor Argunov. 1750–55

*The Anichkov Bridge
in St Petersburg. 1850s.
Coloured lithograph by
Jean Jacottet and Pierre
Regamet after a drawing
by Joseph Charlemagne*

The Alexander Nevsky Lavra
The Cathedral of the Holy Trinity
Designed by Ivan Starov. 1776–90

The Alexander Nevsky Lavra
The Church of the Annunciation
Designed by Domenico Trezzini. 1717–25

Icon: St Alexander Nevsky
Second half of the 19th century

Baroque style with corner churches, two-storey blocks and galleries. Alexander Suvorov, a great army leader, was buried in the oldest building of the monastery, the Church of the Annunciation (1717–25, architect Domenico Trezzini).

The dominant feature of the monastery, given the rank of lavra in 1797, became the majestic Cathedral of the Holy Trinity (1776–90, architect Ivan Starov), designed in the Classical style. The silhouette of the cathedral with its powerful dome and two symmetrical belltowers dominates the panorama of the Neva in this area.

The cemeteries of the Alexander Nevsky Lavra – Lazarevskoye, Tikhvinskoye and Nikolskoye – make up the main part of the St Petersburg necropolis. This is a sort of pantheon where many celebrated figures of Russian history and culture are buried – the great scientist Mikhail Lomonosov, the architects Ivan Starov, Giacomo

Icon: Our Saviour
Second quarter of the 20th century
By the martyr Father Seraphim

Quarenghi, Andrei Voronikhin, Andreyan Zakharov, Carlo Rossi, the sculptors Fedot Shubin, Mikhail Kozlovsky and Ivan Martos at the Lazarevskoye Cemetery; the historian Nikolai Karamzin, the writer Fiodor Dostoyevsky, the composers Mikhail Glinka, Piotr Tchaikovsky and Nikolai Rimsky-Korsakov, as well as many artists, sculptors, actors and other men of culture who contributed to the glory of Russia at the Tikhvinskoye Cemetery.

Patriarch of Muscovy and All the Russias
Alexis II in the Alexander Nevsky Lavra

The Tikhvinskoye Cemetery
Tomb of the Composer Piotr Tchaikovsky
By Pavel Kamensky. 1897

93

The Palaces of the Russian Museum

The State Russian Museum possesses the world's largest collection of Russian art. Founded in 1895, it was opened for visitors in 1898 in the Mikhailovsky Palace (1819–25, architect Carlo Rossi). The State Staircase and the White-Columned Hall have reached us in their original appearance. The decoration of other rooms and halls of the palace built for Grand Duke Mikhail Pavlovich was altered in the course of adapting the building for museum purposes. To accommodate the quickly growing collections, a building was added at

The Mikhailovsky Palace (The Russian Museum)
Designed by Carlo Rossi. 1819–25
Monument to Alexander Pushkin
By Mikhail Anikushin and Vasily Petrov. 1957

the west side and named after its architect, the Benois Block (1914–19, architect Leonty Benois with the participation of Sergei Ovsiannikov). The main façade of the Mikhailovsky Palace affords a view of Arts Square, the compositional centre of which is the monument to Alexander Pushkin unveiled in 1957. The inspired image of the poet was created by the sculptor Mikhail Anikushin.

At the present time the collection of the Russian Museum amounts to about 400,000 exhibits representing national art from the eleventh century to the present day. It includes collections of painting, graphic art, sculpture, decorative and folk art.

The Department of Ancient Russian Art displays outstanding examples of icon-painting, including works by Andrei Rublev, Dionysius and Simon Ushakov,

*The Russian Museum
The White Hall
Designed by Carlo Rossi
First quarter of the 19th century*

*Alexei Venetsianov
Girl in a Kerchief
1830s*

*Karl Briullov
The Last Day of Pompeii. 1833*

Boris Kustodiev
Merchant's Wife at Tea
1918

Victor Vasnetsov
The Knight at Crossroads. 1882

Ivan Shishkin. The Mast Tree Grove. 1898

wooden sculpture, carved stones and bone carvings, embroidery and jewellery. Particularly rich is the collection of art of the eighteenth to twentieth century beginning with the first secular works of the Peter's age – works by Ivan Nikitin, Andrei Matveyev and Ivan Vishniakov to paintings by the avant-garde masters – Kasimir Malevich, Marc Chagall, Pavel Filonov – and other painters of our century.

Museums are similar to icebergs – the greater part of their holdings is hidden from visitors' eyes in their reserves. The Russian Museum is not an exclusion in this respect. The situation, however, changes for the better: on the eve of the 300th Anniversary of St Petersburg the Mikhailovsky (Engineers') Castle and the Marble and Stroganov Palaces have been handed over to the Russian Museum to accommodate and display its representative collections.

Marc Chagall
Promenade
1917–18

Kasimir Malevich
Girls in the Field
1928–32

*Kuzma Petrov-Vodkin
The Virgin of
the Appeasement
of Cruel Hearts
1914–15*

*Pavel Filonov
The Peasant Family
(The Holy Family)
1914*

The Mikhailovsky Castle (1796–1800, architect Vasily Bazhenov and Vincenzo Brenna) was built as a residence of Emperor Paul I, who also contributed to its design. An equestrian statue of Peter the Great (sculptor Bartolomeo Carlo Rastrelli, architect Fiodor Volkov) was set up in front of the south façade in 1800.

The life of the emperor in the building, however, was not long – during the night of 12 March (25 March Old Style) 1801 he was assassinated by conspirators in the state bedroom on the first floor. In 1819 the palace began to house the Main Engineering School and the building, originally named in honour of the Archangel Michael, the patron of Emperor Paul I, was renamed

Emperor Paul I

*The Mikhailovsky (Engineers') Castle. Designed by Vasily Bazhenov and Vincenzo Brenna. 1796–1800
Monument to Peter the Great
By Bartolomeo Carlo Rastrelli. 1743–47*

*View of the Mikhailovsky Castle
from the Summer Gardens*

the Engineers' Castle. The great Russian novelist Fiodor Dostoyevsky studied in this building.

The Marble Palace (1768–85, architect Antonio Rinaldi) was intended by Catherine the Great for her favourite Count Grigory Orlov, but he died before the construction ended. Later the palace became a residence of the last Polish King Stanislaw-August Poniatowski, belonged to Tsesarevich Konstantin Pavlovich, and after him was the property of Grand Duke Konstantin Nikolayevich. The Last owner of the palace was Grand Duke Konstantin K. Romanov, a well-known poet, who signed his verses with the pseudonym K.R.

The Marble Palace is one of the few buildings in St Petersburg where natural stones of different kinds, including various sorts of marble of subtlest gradations,

Empress Maria Feodorovna

103

are used instead of more common plaster. This branch of the Russian Museum now houses a permanent exhibition "Foreign Artists in Russia" and the Peter Ludwig Gallery; temporary exhibitions of contemporary art are also held there.

In front of the east front of the palace stands a monument to the founder of the Russian Museum, Emperor Alexander III, created by the sculptor Paolo Trubetskoi in 1908.

Emperor Alexander III

The Marble Palace. Designed by
Antonio Rinaldi. 1768–85
Monument to Emperor Alexander III
By Paolo Trubetskoi. 1908

Unknown artist. The Marble Palace
First half of the 19th century
Engraving on steel tinted with watercolour

*The Mariinsky Theatre. Designed by Albert Cavos
and Victor Schröter. 1847–1860; 1894–1895*

Around Theatre Square

Theatre Square was shaped in the second half of the eighteenth century. It was the venue for popular festivities, amateur performances and mounted games with theatrical elements. The main feature of the square was the Bolshoi, or Stone Theatre erected by Antonio Rinaldi in 1775–83 and rebuilt in the 1800s by Jean-François Thomas de Thomon. For a long time the Bolshoi ranked with the best theatres of Europe. Its auditorium had three tiers and accommodated about 2,000 spectators. In the course of the past century the building was repaired and reconstructed several times. For a hundred years now it has been occupied by the St Petersburg Conservatory. Many outstanding composers and musicians, including Sergei Prokofyev and Dmitry Shostakovich, studied in it.

Opposite the Conservatory, on the other side of the square stands the Mariinsky Theatre. In 1847–49 a theatre-circus was built on the site. After a fire of 1859 the building was redesigned by Albert Cavos. The new edifice, named the Mariinsky Theatre after Maria Alexandrovna, the wife of Alexander II, was inaugurated in October 1860. The appearance of the building with its imposing, lavishly decorated main façade, took its shape as a result of the reconstruction undertaken in 1894–95 under the supervision of the architect Victor Schröter.

The best achievements of Russian ballet and opera are connected with the Mariinsky (Kirov) Company. Many works by the greatest composers were performed on its stage for the first time. The theatre was and has remained the company incorporating superb casts of

The bell-tower of the Naval Cathedral of St Nicholas

actors, directors and conductors. For several years the ballet company was headed by Maurice Petipa. The Mariinsky Theatre can be proud of its celebrated opera singers Fiodor Chaliapin and Leonid Sobinov, its world-famous dancers Anna Pavlova, Tamara Karsavina, Mathilda Kshesinska, Vaclav Nijinsky, Mikhail Fokine, Galina Ulanova and others.

The Griboyedov and Kriukov Canals are within a stone's throw from Theatre Square. Rivers and canals are an integral part of the historically formed image of St Petersburg. Smaller waterways perhaps even better than its streets and avenues reflect the specific layout of the city and even its spiritual atmosphere. The perception of architectural and artistic monuments is enhanced by their neighbourhood to water expanses and granite embankments.

The Griboyedov Canal combines the features of a man-made urban waterway with a natural picturesque quality, adding much variety to the regular layout of St Petersburg. Its embankments belong to the most expressive and poetic sights in the city. The narrow riverbed, the winding banks, the arches of bridges and the old mansions reflected in the smooth waters, all

The Tsar's box

adds to its special enchantment. At the spot where the canal loops around the three Podyacheskaya Streets, a suspension bridge intended for pedestrians and decorated with companion sculptures of lions suddenly appears after an abrupt turn. The Lion Bridge was constructed in 1825–26 by the engineer Wilhelm von Tretter, and the lions concealing the ends of the suspending chains were produced by the sculptor Pavel Sokolov.

Not far from the intersection of the Griboyedov Kriukov Canals there soars the four-tiered bell-tower of the Naval Cathedral of St Nicholas. The graceful silhouette of the bell-tower crowned with a small spire harmoniously blends with the picturesque view of the Kriukov Canal. The Cathedral of St Nicholas, detached from the bell-tower, is a masterpiece of Russian Baroque architecture (1753–62, architect Savva

The Kriukov Canal. View of the bell-tower of the Naval Cathedral of St Nicholas

Chevakinsky). Cruciform in plan, the five-domed cathedral is remarkable for its expressive volumes and shapes. The dense bundles of columns, the elaborate window surrounds and lavish moulded decoration highlight by their whiteness the blue background of the walls. A notable feature of the upper church of the cathedral is the beautiful iconostasis carved by the master craftsman Ignaty Kanayev.

At the spot where the Kriukov Canal empties into the Moika River, stands the monumental brick building the fronts of which are pierced with high arches. It stands on the man-made island known as "New Holland" which once served as a warehouse for storing and seasoning ship timber. The waterway leading to the inside of New Holland from the Moika, is adorned with a majestic triumphal arch (1765–80, architect Jean-Baptiste Vallin de la Mothe). This is one of the most romantic corners of St Petersburg.

◀ *The domes of the Naval Cathedral of St Nicholas*

The Naval Cathedral of St Nicholas Designed by Savva Chevakinsky. 1753–62

The Palace Bridge

The Northern Capital

The granite city of glory and disaster
Anna Akhmatova

How can the phenomenon of St Petersburg be described? It is the city of a universally recognized, unique beauty. The city of eventful, dramatic history. It is a rather young city, in comparison with Rome and Paris, London and Amsterdam – merely about three hundred years old.

The birth of a new capital in the huge country was of course an epoch-making event. It was to mark the temporal boundary between the old Russian Middle Ages and the two hundred years of new Russian history, known as the St Petersburg period. The city founded by

Peter the Great in 1703 on the Baltic Sea, was conceived from the very beginning as "a window to Europe", and it also served as a wide door for foreigners coming to Russia. It played a decisive role in the modernization of the country, in its transformation into a great European and world state.

Unlike ancient Russian towns, St Petersburg was not formed spontaneously, little by little in the course of centuries, but was built within a strikingly short period. Its rationally worked out regular plan was based on the ideas of Peter the Great himself. The northern capital on the banks of the wide Neva was conceived according to European standards, yet built with a truly Russian sweep. The entire country took part in its creation. And almost entire Europe too. Architects, artists and scholars, craftsmen, traders and sailors, all

View of the Peter and Paul Fortress
from the Trinity Bridge

115

came to the city from abroad. The age – old traditions and contemporary experience of the Western civilization and town-planning were not only quickly mastered in St Petersburg, but were immediately translated into practical results. In this way a unique urban, social and cultural phenomenon – a typically Russian city with its own, distinctly European appearance, character and aura – was taking shape.

The essential feature of Russian history is a colonization of new territories. The eastern Slavs and later the Russians were used to live side by side with other tribes and peoples, mainly as peaceful neighbours. This shaped a characteristic feature of the Russian national character – a forbearance and a respect to things foreign to its nature, an ability to understand such alien things and to borrow freely what is necessary, to enrich itself without losing its national identity. It is largely thanks to a "universal responsiveness", as Fyodor Dostoyevsky defined this quality, that such an extensive and multinational state as Russia, the culminating accomplishment of which was St Petersburg, could emerge and develop. The city did not become a tower of Babylon or a casual conglomerate of different cultures. It acquired a new kind of unity and integrity, with its inhabitants feeling themselves as "Petersburgers", independently of their nationality and transforming the predominant European styles of Baroque or Neo-Classicism into the "Russian Baroque" or "Russian Classicism".

At the same time this city is an implemented utopia. It is inseparably linked with Peter's reforms and the giant personality of the Tsar-Reformer. All the contradictory attitudes to the reforms were equally applied to St Petersburg. It was thought to be the centre of evil and crime, a symbol of popular suffering, violence, all-devastating willful power, but it was also regarded as the triumph of reason, of Peter's genius which opened up new horizons of Russian history, a symbol of a special

The Winter Canal

View of Palace Square

beauty of the rational mode of life, an ideal city, a city-idea and a city-myth.

One could feel either love or hate to St Petersburg, but hardly anybody could be indifferent to it. The emphasized European aspect of the new capital on the Neva evoked contradictory moods in Russians. An admiration for a beautiful city previously unseen in this country was combined with a keen feeling of its artificial and foreign essence, its estrangement from the native roots. Sometimes this resulted in an outspoken neglect of the capital which had emerged on the swampy Finnish marshes and seemingly was ready to disappear as a mirage. However, even this "negative aspect" of the St Petersburg myth was creatively transformed so that it yielded great results in literature and the fine arts.

Although St Petersburg has a relatively short history, it has become the subject of numerous myths and legends. The ancient Russian capitals, Kiev and Moscow, cannot rival St Petersburg in this respect. The city as a "sign", the city as a "text", with an abundance of its readings and connotations; the city eulogized in inspired poetry and in prose, reflected in different ways in graphic art and in painting, it constantly stirs one's thoughts, inspires imagination and creativity. The culture of St Petersburg has an especial atmosphere about it stimulating a self-reflection, an involvement into the study of the amazing phenomenon of the city and brooding over its positive and negative aspects. Its great, if contradictory, role in Russian and world culture has already been realized for a century and a half, but its mystery still continues to trouble us today.

The crest of St Petersburg includes two crossing stocked anchors with their arms turned upwards. This looks like a paraphrase of the coat-of-arms of Vatican featuring keys from Paradise, preserved by the St Apostle Peter. In both cases "keys" are represented, but in the former case keys from the heavenly kingdom are meant, and in the latter from the earthly "paradise". St Petersburg as a sea and river port of Russia was a sort of key opening a door to the western world, to the European civilization – Peter's idea of "paradise".

By the way, it was in this city that all Russian revolutions began – utopian attempts to establish the heavenly kingdom on the earth. St Petersburg was founded by the "revolutionary on the throne", and the city of Peter the Great grew to become "a citadel of the three revolutions".

View of St Isaac's and Decembrists' Square

"New Holland". Designed by Savva Chevakinsky and Jean-Baptiste Vallin de la Mothe. 1765–80

Erected on the bones of many thousands of its builders, the city was a witness to and participant in great and tragic events: palatial coups and the Decembrists' mutiny, the development of the Russian industry and the birth of superb national literature, "Bloody Sunday" in 1905, the February and October Revolutions in 1917, that "shook the world", the "great terror" of the 1930s, the heroic exploits of soldiers during the war, the tragedy of the siege for 900 days which took away about a million of people, the devastation of the Communist Empire...

To understand the "soul of St Petersburg", one must bear in mind two highly important factors connected with its natural environment.

This city is the northernmost metropolis in the world. It is situated at the same latitude as Greenland and Alaska. It is not always pleasant, of course, but thanks to the long polar day "the Palmyra of the North" may boast a natural miracle which is one of its most brilliant features – the White Nights.

Another pride of St Petersburg is the Neva River. If the assertion that the Volga is the main waterway of Russia is right, then the Neva is certainly the main thoroughfare of St Petersburg. The wide and full-watered river is quite short – only seventy-four kilometers divide its source at Lake Ladoga from its estuary where it empties into the Gulf of Finland of the Baltic Sea. And for about thirty kilometers the river carries its waters through the city forming with its numerous branches and canals a fascinating poetic realm including lovely islands and islets.

However, the beautiful Neva has a capricious character, which brought to the city a lot of disasters. St Petersburg as such was formed in a struggle with hostile elements, in overcoming unfavourable natural conditions. The main danger for the city located on the low banks came from frequent floods.

There was a constant struggle between the city and the elements for some time, but the dynamic process of urbanization soon transformed the natural landscape. Architecture began to blend harmoniously with

Grigory Rasputin

The Yusupov Palace. Here monarchist conspirators assassinated the royal favourite Grigory Rasputin in 1916

*The cruiser "Aurora"
near the building of
the Nakhimov Naval
Cadet School*

the subjugated water element gradually shaping the distinctive image of the city. Canals clad in granite embankments, gardens with man-made ponds and fountains largely improved the ecological situation and gave a more "aesthetic" view to the dull scenery of the flat banks.

The dense building of historical areas of the city was limited to two planes – the vertical one, forming the unbroken front of façades and the horizontal one defined by the admissible upper limit of height. Before the early twentieth century it was not allowed to put up secular buildings higher than the Imperial Winter Palace (23.5 metres). It made a common construction even more monolithic and enabled architects to highlight tall landmarks making the city's outline still more picturesque.

The main building materials in St Petersburg were brick and plaster. This made the refashioning of façades to cater changing tastes easier. Therefore buildings in the historical part of the city frequently have several chronological "layers". This peculiar feature typical of

The Chesme Church
Designed by Yury Velten
1777–80

St Petersburg probably deprives its architecture of the aura of originality to some extent, but it vividly records all its historical zigzags.

Numerous forecasts about the imminent end of the city, about its "way to nowhere" cast a dark shadow on its image. And seemingly safeguarding the city of the Holy Apostle Peter from his participation in the forthcoming bloody events, the name of the heavenly patron was replaced by the earthly name of the city's founder – between 1914 and 1924 the city was known as Petrograd. This gloomy decade saw the defeat of Russia in the First World War, the Bolshevik coup of 25 October 1917 and the fratricidal Civil War. In March 1918 the city lost its status of the capital of Russia. Petrograd stood forlorn and desolated, as if it had been completely exhausted during its short lifetime. The year 1924, when the city was given the new name of Leningrad, saw the beginning of the new, socialist era with its distinctive ideology and specific morals.

However, it was Leningrad that accomplished a great feat of redemption during the War of 1941–45. The city withstood the enemy's blockade for 900 days and nights, having lost a million of its inhabitants who perished from hunger, cold and bombardments. The city which did not surrender once again struck the world by its powerful spirit and undaunted courage.

The Cathedral of St Prince Vladimir
The miraculous icon of Our Lady
of Kazan. 16th century

The Cathedral of St Prince Vladimir. Designed by Mikhail Zemtsov, Antonio Rinaldi and Ivan Starov. 1740–89

The Smolny Cathedral. Designed by Francesco Bartolomeo Rastrelli, 1748–64; Vasily Stasov, 1832–35

The date which marked a new period in the life of the city was 6 September 1991 when, after a general referendum, its former, original and authentic name of St Petersburg has been revived.

Looking at the beautiful city lying on the banks of the quiet yet ever flowing Neva, one is sure to believe that St Petersburg has not only the glorious past, but a great future too.

The Okhta Bridge ▶

Tsarskoye Selo

At the beginning of the eighteenth century the site of the present-day town of Pushkin was occupied by a Swedish farmstead, Saari Mojs ("elevated place"). In 1708 Peter the Great presented it to Catherine, his wife. After 1725 the farmstead was gradually developed into a magnificent Imperial residence called Tsarskoye Selo (Tsar's Village).

In 1717–23 Johann Braunstein put up a small stone palace there. In 1752–56, the architect Francesco Bartolomeo Rastrelli, employed by Empress Elizabeth Petrovna, united separate parts of the palatial complex into a grand entity, with an imposing and luxurious

The Great (Catherine) Palace. Designed by Francesco Bartolomeo Rastrelli. 1752–56

façade (300 metres long), a grand staircase and a suite of state rooms richly adorned with gilded carving, mirrors and amber. The reign of Catherine the Great saw the construction of the Church and Zubov wings of the Great Palace, the Cold Baths with the Agate Rooms, the Hanging Garden and the Cameron Gallery. Works by Charles Cameron, a connoisseur of ancient classical art and refined architect, are marked by a wide gamut of impressions, from austere monumentality to airy lightness and inimitable decorative elegance.

The architecture of the Tsarskoye Selo palaces perfectly blends with the parks and gardens surrounding the residence. The Catherine Park is adorned with all kinds of pavilions (the Hermitage, the Grotto, the Admiralty, the "Creaky" Summerhouse, the Ruin Folly, etc.), as well as decorative structures, whimsical bridges and pieces of sculpture. In the centre of the great pond

The Great Palace

stands the Chesme (Orlov) Column (1774–76. architect Antonio Rinaldi) erected to commemorate the victory of the Russian fleet over the Turks off Chesme in the Aegean Sea in 1770.

No less picturesque are the landscapes of the Alexander Park where numerous exotic and Romantic structures have survived: the Great Caprice, the Cross Bridge, the Arsenal, the Chapelle, the Pensionary Stables, the Chinese Village and others.

Between 1792 and 1800 Giacomo Quarenghi erected the Alexander Palace in the style of austere Classicism. The new palace was intended for the nephew of Catherine the Great, the future Emperor Alexander the Great.

In 1811 the Lyceum, a special school for children of the nobility, was established at Tsarskoye Selo. It became particularly famous because the great poet Pushkin studied there until 1817. In 1900 a monument to the poet by the sculptor Robert Bach was installed in the Lyceum Garden. The Memorial Museum functioning in the former Lyceum building has been founded in 1949.

The Great Palace
The Blue Chinese
Drawing Room
Designed by
Charles Cameron
1781–83

The Great Palace. The Great (Throne) Hall
Designed by Francesco Bartolomeo Rastrelli. 1750s

The Chinese ("Creaky") Summerhouse.
Designed by Yury Velten. 1778–82

The Catherine Park. The Cameron Gallery
Designed by Charles Cameron. 1783–87

*The Great Palace. Designed by
Charles Cameron. 1782–86*

Pavlovsk

The town of Pavlovsk was founded on the Slavianka River in 1777 as an estate of Grand Duke Pavel Petrovich (the future Emperor Paul I). Later, in 1782–86, the architect Charles Cameron built a palace there. During the same period a landscaped park with numerous ponds, elegant bridges and pavilions was laid out. The stately and integral ensemble of Pavlovsk was created in the course of a half of a century.

The Pavlovsk Palace, a fine example of the architecture of Russian Classicism, is remarkable for its stately appearance and elegance of its decor. The main

*The Centaur Bridge. Designed by Charles Cameron
and Andrei Voronikhin. 1799–1805*

building, together with arc-shaped galleries leading to the wings (rebuilt in the 1790s by Vincenzo Brenna) forms a large open courtyard. After a fire of 1803 the palace was restored under the supervision of Andrei Voronikhin.

In 1838 Pavlovsk was connected with St Petersburg by the first Russian railway. During summer months the concert hall near the Pavlovsk Station (it was burned down during the Second World War) became the centre of musical life in the capital.

Today the palace-museum and the poetic parks of Pavlovsk are a favourite recreation place of the inhabitants of St Petersburg and visitors to the city. Following the tradition, concerts of classical music are held in the Grecian Hall of the palace.

*The Great
Palace*

*The Great Palace
The Egyptian Vestibule
Designed by Charles Cameron, 1780s;
Andrei Voronikhin, 1803*

*The Visconti Bridge
Designed by
Andrei Voronikhin
1808*

*The Temple of Friendship
Designed by Charles Cameron. 1780–82*

The Chinese Palace. Designed by
Antonio Rinaldi. 1762–68

Oranienbaum

At the beginning of the eighteenth century a small farmstead on the southern shore of the Gulf of Finland, opposite Kotlin Island, was granted by Peter the Great to his favourite, Prince Alexander Menshikov. From 1710 onwards it was known as Oranienbaum. Legend has it that on the territory of the estate presented to Menshikov there was a hothouse with orange trees. Each of the trees had the inscription: Oranienbaum. Peter the Great found this fact amusing and gave this name to the estate. In 1785 a representation of the orange tree with fruit similar to oranges became part of the crest of Oranienbaum.

The formation of the palace-and-park ensemble was started at Oranienbaum in 1710–27 when the Great Palace in the Baroque style was built to designs by the architects Giovanni Fontana and Johann Schädel. In 1762–80 it was redesigned by Antonio Rinaldi. The arc-shaped galleries connect the central block of the palace with the two structures surmounted with domes (the Church and the Japanese Pavilion). The elaborately decorated staircase descends to the regular Lower Park provided with a canal leading to the sea.

After Prince Menshikov had been exiled to Siberia in 1727, Oranienbaum became the state property

Sculptural group "The Three Graces"
by the Chinese Palace

141

Emperor Peter III

and in 1743–61 it served as a summer residence of the heir, Grand Duke Piotr Fiodorovich (the future Emperor Peter III). This period saw the creation of the Upper Park, where Antonio Rinaldi built the Palace of Peter III (1758–62), and when Catherine the Great came to the throne he put up the Chinese Palace (1762–68) and the Sliding Hill Pavilion (1762–74).

The gem of the Oranienbaum Open-Air Museum is the Chinese Palace, a unique example of the Rococo style. The design of its state rooms which have preserved their original decor, is based on motifs borrowed from Chinese art. The palace has a fine display of paintings by artists of the Venetian School, of Russian and Western European porcelain and furniture as well as works of Oriental decorative art.

The Great Palace. The Japanese Pavilion
Designed by Antonio Rinaldi. 1762–80

*The Sliding Hill Pavilion. Designed
by Antonio Rinaldi. 1762–74*

*The "Honourary Gate"
of the Palace of Peter III*

*The Great Cascade and the Great Palace
at Peterhof. By Vasily Sadovnikov. 1845*

Peterhof

eter the Great made strenuous efforts to develop the environs of his new capital, especially the shores of the Gulf of Finland. As a result of his projects magnificent palace-and-park complexes of Strelna, Peterhof and Oranienbaum were created there.

The architecture of that time was based on creative assimilation of foreign accomplishments, on the mastery of the architectural principles of the Renaissance, Baroque and Classicism. The aesthetic tastes which were new for Russia were transmitted by foreign architects, builders, painters and sculptors. The founder of St Petersburg and his successors invited them from different European countries. On familiarizing themselves with

*Fountain statue: Samson Rending Open the Jaws
of the Lion. By Mikhail Kozlovsky. 1802*

Russian life the foreign architects faced with the rich experience of local builders and with specific tastes of their commissioners. The newly introduced artistic orientation should not be regarded as a neglect of the national traditions, because its was precisely the mastery of European cultural achievements that was vital and urgent for the development of the country.

Peter the Great founded Peterhof in 1705. The building of the celebrated palace-and-park ensemble began in the 1710s. Its compositional centre is the Great Palace which towers on the natural terrace facing the Gulf of Finland. The original two-storey palace was created in 1714–25 (architects Johann Braunstein, Mikhail Zemtsov, Jean-Baptiste Le Blond, Niccolo Michetti). In 1745–55 the building was demolished and rebuilt by Francesco Bartolomeo Rastrelli along the lines of the Elizabethan Baroque. The state interiors of the palace – the Throne Room, the Study of Peter the Great faced

*The Great Palace
Designed by
Johann Braunstein,
Mikhail Zemtsov,
Jean-Baptiste
Le Blond, Niccolo
Michetti, 1714–25;
Francesco
Bartolomeo
Rastrelli, 1745–55*

The Great Cascade
The West Cascade Staircase

The Great Cascade (The Pool). Niccolo Michetti, 1721–25;
Andrei Stakenschneider, 1854

with oak panels (carved by Nicholas Pineau), the Chinese Lobbies, the Portrait Hall, the White Dining Room, etc. – are outstanding examples of architecture and decorative art.

Parks play the most important part in the ensemble – the Upper Gardens with five fountains on the south side and the Lower Park with the largest complex of fountains on the north side overlooking the sea. The Great Grotto with the Great Cascade framing it forms a decorative base for the palace. The Great Cascade, decorated with numerous fountains, gilded bronze statues, bas-reliefs, vases and bowls, descends towards the pool in the centre of which stands the monumental statue-fountain "Samson Rending Open the Jaws of the Lion" (1802, sculptor Mikhail Kozlovsky). A powerful jet of water spurts out of the lion's jaw to the height of twenty metres.

The Lower Park is adorned with a great number of different fountains as well as with the Marly Palace and the Hermitage Pavilion built to the design of Johann Braunstein in the early 1720s. On the bank of the Gulf of Finland stands the Monplaisir complex (1714–23, architects Jean-Baptiste Le Blond, Niccolo Michetti, Johann Braunstein, Mikhail Zemtsov, etc.). The rooms and galleries diverging from the central stately Hall display decorative objects of the early eighteenth century and paintings by Western European masters from the collection of Peter the Great.

The Cottage Palace was built in the landscaped Alexandria Park in 1826–29 by the architect Adam Menelaws as a summer residence for the family of Emperor Nicholas I in the vein of mediaeval English structures.

In 1918 the palaces of Peterhof became museums. During the occupation of the town from 23 September 1941 to 19 January 1944 the Nazi soldiers plundered the museums, ruined the palaces, cut out trees or dug out trenches in the parks, destroyed fountains, water supply system, canals and sluices.

Restoration work was started even before the end of the war, soon after the liberation of the town. Today

The Roman Fountain. Designed by Ivan Blank and Ivan Davydov, 1738–39; Francesco Bartolomeo Rastrelli, 1763

The Great Palace. The Oak Staircase
Designed by
Jean-Baptiste Le Blond
and Nicolas Pineau
1714–1725

The Great Palace
The Oak Study of Peter the Great
Designed by Jean-Baptiste Le Blond,
Johann Braunstein and Nicolas Pineau. 1718–20

The Great Palace
The State Staircase
Designed by
Francesco
Bartolomeo Rastrelli
1750s

Empress Elizabeth Petrovna

**The Great Palace. The Throne Room
Designed by Francesco Bartolomeo
Rastrelli, 1749–52; Yury Velten, 1777–79**

*The Blue Drawing Room. Designed by Francesco
Bartolomeo Rastrelli, 1750s; Andrei Stakenschneider, 1844*

*The Great Palace. The Audience Room
Designed by Francesco Bartolomeo Rastrelli. 1749–55* ▶

◀ *The Upper Gardens*
H. Ritter, Georg Schweiger
Fountain: Neptune
1650–58; 1798–99

The Lower Park. The Palace of Marly
Designed by Johann Friedrich Braunstein. 1720–24

The Lower Park. The Hermitage Pavilion
Designed by Johann Friedrich Braunstein. 1721–25

The Upper Gardens. The Oak Fountain
Designed by Ivan Blank, Ivan Davydov
and Bartolomeo Carlo Rastrelli. 1733–35

The Lower Park. The Monplaisir complex
Designed by Johann Friedrich Braunstein. 1714–23

The Palace of Monplaisir. Designed by Johann
Friedrich Braunstein and Philippe Pillement. The Hall

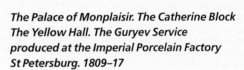

The Palace of Monplaisir. The Catherine Block
The Yellow Hall. The Guryev Service
produced at the Imperial Porcelain Factory
St Petersburg. 1809–17

The Monplaisir Palace
The Catherine Block
Designed by
Francesco Bartolomeo
Rastrelli, 1748–49;
Giacomo Quarenghi,
1785–86

The Alexandria Park
The Gothic Chapel
("The Church of
St Alexander Nevsky")
Designed by Adam Menelaws,
Joseph Charlemagne. 1831–34

The Cathedral of the SS Apostles
Peter and Paul. Designed by
Nikolai Sultanov. 1894, 1905

a significant part of the palace and park ensemble and fountains has been restored (architects-restorers Alexander Hessen, Andrei Ol, Vasily Savkov and Yevgeniya Kazanskaya).

The unique complex of fascinating water cascades and fountains, resplendent parks, palaces and pavilions turned Peterhof into a real paradise, the "Russian Versailles", as Peter dreamed.

The Cottage Palace
The Dining Room

Empress Alexandra Feodorovna

The Alexandria Park. The Cottage Palace
Designed by Adam Menelaws. 1826–29

Contents